Quilter's
DESK DIARY
2011

Welcome to 2011
Stay organized in style with *The Quilter's Desk Diary 2011*. Illustrated throughout with beautiful photographs of inspirational quilts from the most talented of quiltmakers, each week-to-view diary page has plenty of room for your own personal notes. If you want to find out more about any of the quiltmakers featured, turn to the back of the book for information about them and the books they have written.

D&C
David and Charles
www.rucraft.co.uk

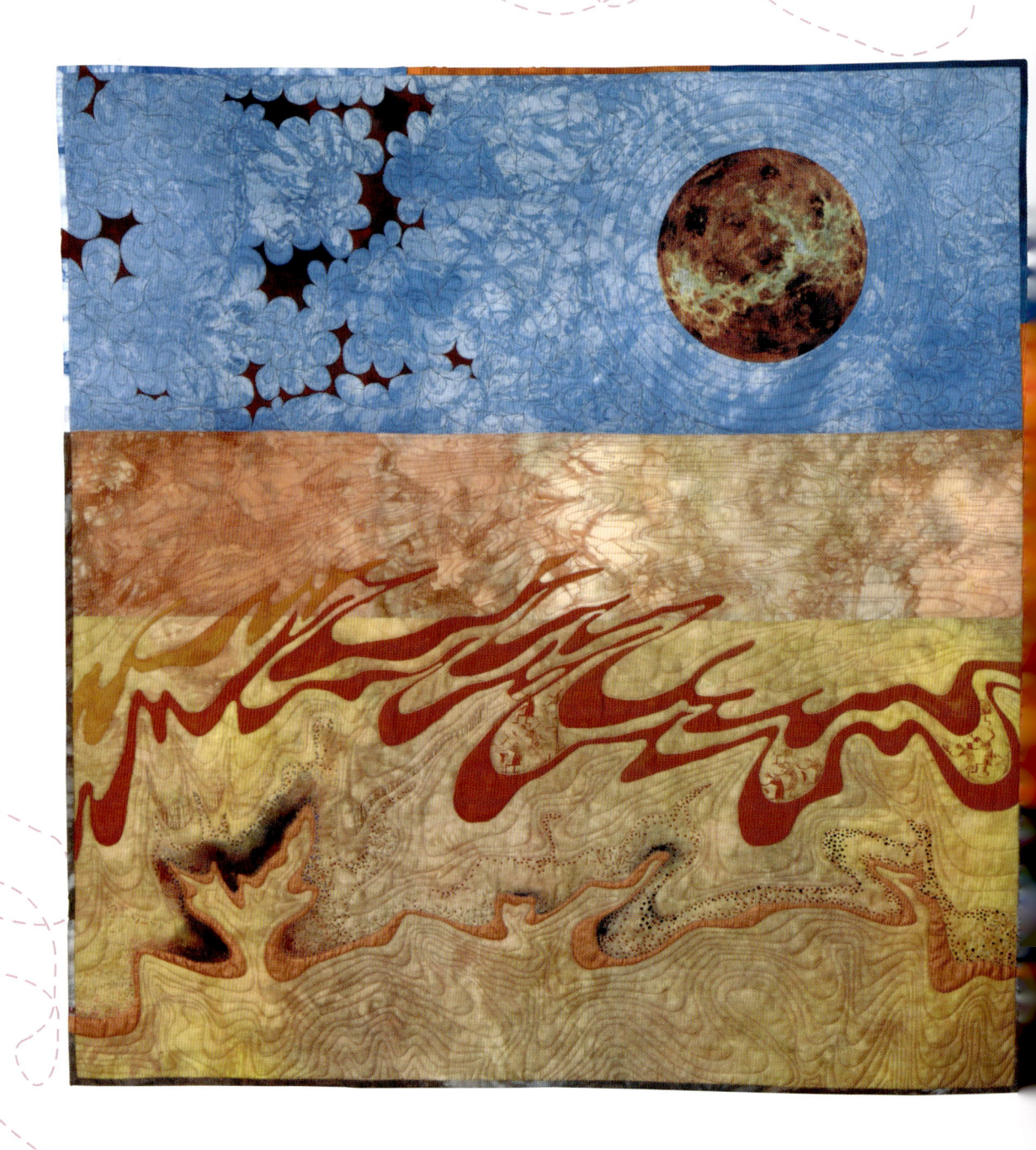

Dreamtime

What better inspiration for a new year of quiltmaking than this stunning quilt by Linda Kershall from *The Painted Quilt*, a book that shows how you can combine paints, pens, pastels, dyes, image transfer and fusible web to produce intricate textile effects on quilted fabrics. Finished size: 38 x 39½in.

December/January

27
Monday

28
Tuesday

29
Wednesday

30
Thursday

31
Friday

New Year's Day

1
Saturday

2
Sunday

DECEMBER						
M	T	W	T	F	S	S
		1	2	3	4	5
6	7	8	9	10	11	12
13	14	15	16	17	18	19
20	21	22	23	24	25	26
27	28	29	30	31		

Peacock Windows

In *Cathedral Window Quilts*, Lynne Edwards explores this classic folded technique and a wealth of variations on it. In the wall hanging above, she has used Secret Garden squares (a four-petal variation) in the centre of the design and surrounded it with classic Cathedral Window squares. Finished size: 38 x 38in.

January

Bank Holiday (UK)

3
Monday

4
Tuesday

5
Wednesday

6
Thursday

7
Friday

8
Saturday

9
Sunday

JANUARY

M	T	W	T	F	S	S
					1	2
3	4	5	6	7	8	9
10	11	12	13	14	15	16
17	18	19	20	21	22	23
24	25	26	27	28	29	30
31						

String Stars And Spiders' Webs

Strings, traditionally, were the odd pieces left over from dressmaking. Of varying lengths and widths, they could be sewn to a foundation by a thrifty seamstress to form blocks for a quilt. Inspired by this tradition, Carolyn Forster created this interlocking design for *The Quiltmakers*. Finished size: 76½ x 76½in.

January

10
Monday

11
Tuesday

12
Wednesday

13
Thursday

14
Friday

15
Saturday

16
Sunday

JANUARY

M	T	W	T	F	S	S
					1	2
3	4	5	6	7	8	9
10	11	12	13	14	15	16
17	18	19	20	21	22	23
24	25	26	27	28	29	30
31						

Sparkling Gemstones

In Jelly Roll Quilts, Pam and Nicky Lintott present a collection of quilt designs that can be made from just one roll of the pre-cut 2½in fabric strips. This quilt is great for using large-scale prints, and a light stone-coloured background makes the fabric 'gems' stand out even more. Finished size: 58 x 76in.

January

Martin Luther King Day (US)

17
Monday

18
Tuesday

19
Wednesday

20
Thursday

21
Friday

22
Saturday

23
Sunday

JANUARY

M	T	W	T	F	S	S
					1	2
3	4	5	6	7	8	9
10	11	12	13	14	15	16
17	18	19	20	21	22	23
24	25	26	27	28	29	30
31						

Dancing Angels

Mandy Shaw, the designer of this quilt, is a self-confessed master of quick and fast techniques. In her book *Quilt Yourself Gorgeous*, she has great ways to save you time without compromising on charm. Her beautiful designs are embellished with hand-stitching, buttons and braids. Finished size: 52 x 52in.

January

24
Monday

25
Tuesday

Australia Day (Aus)

26
Wednesday

27
Thursday

28
Friday

29
Saturday

30
Sunday

JANUARY

M	T	W	T	F	S	S
					1	2
3	4	5	6	7	8	9
10	11	12	13	14	15	16
17	18	19	20	21	22	23
24	25	26	27	28	29	30
31						

Magic Lantern

In *Making Scrap Quilts to Use It Up!*, Lynne Edwards presents endless ways of making quilts from your fabric stash. Here, a lantern block was made from two different fabrics, and a border of 60-degree triangles was the solution when no piece of fabric remained of sufficient length to make a framing border. Finished size: 47 x 50in.

January/February

31
Monday

1
Tuesday

2
Wednesday

Chinese New Year

3
Thursday

4
Friday

5
Saturday

6
Sunday

FEBRUARY

M	T	W	T	F	S	S
	1	2	3	4	5	6
7	8	9	10	11	12	13
14	15	16	17	18	19	20
21	22	23	24	25	26	27
28						

Starry Quilt

In *Scrap Quilt Sensation*, Katharine Guerrier showcases colourful quilt designs that can be made from fabric leftovers. This sampler quilt provides a twist on a quilting tradition. Sixteen blocks are featured, and, for added colour and movement, Katharine has skewed the blocks and replaced the usual sashing border with a saw-tooth pattern. Finished size: 52½ x 52½in.

February

7
Monday

8
Tuesday

9
Wednesday

10
Thursday

11
Friday

12
Saturday

13
Sunday

FEBRUARY

M	T	W	T	F	S	S
	1	2	3	4	5	6
7	8	9	10	11	12	13
14	15	16	17	18	19	20
21	22	23	24	25	26	27
28						

Be My Valentine

The Jelly Roll Challenge was an international competition held in 2008/2009 to find the best and most creative use of just one jelly roll. The twelve best quilt designs were published in *Jelly Roll Inspirations*, compiled by Pam and Nicky Lintott, and the winning quilt was this romantic design by Helen Allinson. Finished size: 72 x 72in.

February

Valentine's Day

14
Monday

15
Tuesday

16
Wednesday

17
Thursday

18
Friday

19
Saturday

20
Sunday

FEBRUARY

M	T	W	T	F	S	S
	1	2	3	4	5	6
7	8	9	10	11	12	13
14	15	16	17	18	19	20
21	22	23	24	25	26	27
28						

Up, Out And Into The Light

Tessellating patterns – identical units that interlock with one another – are a fantastic resource for quilts. This pattern is called Porter's Puzzle after its creator Christine Porter, the author of *Tessellation Quilts*. Here the pattern continues out to the sashing, and the gold machine quilting that radiates outwards enhances the effect. Finished size: 39½ x 39½in.

February

Presidents' Day (US)

21 Monday

22 Tuesday

23 Wednesday

24 Thursday

25 Friday

26 Saturday

27 Sunday

FEBRUARY

M	T	W	T	F	S	S
	1	2	3	4	5	6
7	8	9	10	11	12	13
14	15	16	17	18	19	20
21	22	23	24	25	26	27
28						

Saw-Tooth

In *Making Welsh Quilts*, Mary Jenkins and Clare Claridge explore the striking similarities between Welsh wool quilts and Amish designs. This quilt replicates the central section of a late 19th century wool quilt. The saw-tooth border, in which all the red triangles go anti-clockwise around the central square, gives this simple quilt a great sense of dynamism. Finished size: 24 x 24in.

February/March

28
Monday

1
Tuesday

2
Wednesday

3
Thursday

4
Friday

5
Saturday

6
Sunday

MARCH

M	T	W	T	F	S	S
	1	2	3	4	5	6
7	8	9	10	11	12	13
14	15	16	17	18	19	20
21	22	23	24	25	26	27
28	29	30	31			

Takusan Tsugi

Takusan Tsugi means 'many patch', a fitting name for this richly-coloured lap quilt made from an Oriental charm pack. The narrow black sashing allows for normally clashing colours and designs to sit quite happily together. The quilt's designers are Julia Davis and Anne Muxworthy, authors of *Easy Japanese Quilt Style*. Finished size: 39 x 54in.

March

7
Monday

Shrove Tuesday

8
Tuesday

9
Wednesday

10
Thursday

11
Friday

12
Saturday

13
Sunday

MARCH

M	T	W	T	F	S	S
	1	2	3	4	5	6
7	8	9	10	11	12	13
14	15	16	17	18	19	20
21	22	23	24	25	26	27
28	29	30	31			

Purple Prose

In *Quilts Beneath Your Feet*, Christine Porter has created a quilt collection inspired by the strong similarity between decorative floor tiles and traditional patchwork patterns. She found this design (a perfect 54.40 or Fight block) in the entrance hall of the Clifton Club, a traditional gentleman's club near her home in Bristol, England. Finished size: 44 x 44in.

March

14
Monday

15
Tuesday

16
Wednesday

St Patrick's Day

17
Thursday

18
Friday

19
Saturday

20
Sunday

MARCH

M	T	W	T	F	S	S
	1	2	3	4	5	6
7	8	9	10	11	12	13
14	15	16	17	18	19	20
21	22	23	24	25	26	27
28	29	30	31			

Julia's Quilt

Dutch quilter Petra Prins was inspired by antique English medallion quilts to create this stunning design for *The Quiltmakers*. Made from Japanese reproduction fabrics, it has a large rose border design as its focal point. The traditional pattern is simple to make; it begins with a centre block and borders are added one by one. Finished size: 56½ x 56½in.

March

21
Monday

22
Tuesday

23
Wednesday

24
Thursday

25
Friday

26
Saturday

27
Sunday

MARCH

M	T	W	T	F	S	S
	1	2	3	4	5	6
7	8	9	10	11	12	13
14	15	16	17	18	19	20
21	22	23	24	25	26	27
28	29	30	31			

Blue And Lime Delight

This was the very first quilt made by Barbara Chainey using the innovative cutting plan devised for her book *Fast Quilts from Fat Quarters*, which helps quilters take any number of fat quarters and quickly turn them into unique quilts. Finished size: 41 x 51in.

March/April

28 Monday

29 Tuesday

30 Wednesday

31 Thursday

1 Friday

2 Saturday

Mother's Day (UK)

3 Sunday

APRIL
M	T	W	T	F	S	S
				1	2	3
4	5	6	7	8	9	10
11	12	13	14	15	16	17
18	19	20	21	22	23	24
25	26	27	28	29	30	

Stepping Out

The Quilters' Guild Heritage Collection is the largest national collection of patchwork and quilting in the UK. In *The Quilters' Guild Collection*, 12 quiltmakers were invited to design a modern interpretation of a traditional piece. This design by Jo Rednall is a contemporary take on a Red and White quilt. Finished size: 33 x 35in.

April

4
Monday

5
Tuesday

6
Wednesday

7
Thursday

8
Friday

9
Saturday

10
Sunday

APRIL

M	T	W	T	F	S	S
				1	2	3
4	5	6	7	8	9	10
11	12	13	14	15	16	17
18	19	20	21	22	23	24
25	26	27	28	29	30	

Lady Of The Lake

Marsha McCloskey has collected and recorded hundreds of Feathered Star blocks, and she shares her love, passion and expertise of these beautiful designs in *The Quiltmakers*. This quilt has a Le Moyne Star as its central block, surrounded by side and corner units, each edged with strip-pieced feather units. Finished size: 41 x 41in.

April

11
Monday

12
Tuesday

13
Wednesday

14
Thursday

15
Friday

16
Saturday

17
Sunday

			APRIL			
M	T	W	T	F	S	S
				1	2	3
4	5	6	7	8	9	10
11	12	13	14	15	16	17
18	19	20	21	22	23	24
25	26	27	28	29	30	

Hexagon Hip Hop

Layer Cake, Jelly Roll and Charm Quilts, by Pam and Nicky Lintott, features 17 quick and clever designs to help you get the most from your pre-cut fabric bundles. Just one layer cake is used for this bright quilt; half hexagons are sewn into vertical rows for easy machine piecing, and the fabric off cuts are used for the border. Finished size: 56 x 62in.

April

18 Monday

19 Tuesday

20 Wednesday

21 Thursday

Good Friday (UK, Aus)

22 Friday

23 Saturday

Easter Sunday

24 Sunday

APRIL

M	T	W	T	F	S	S
				1	2	3
4	5	6	7	8	9	10
11	12	13	14	15	16	17
18	19	20	21	22	23	24
25	26	27	28	29	30	

Johnsons' Floor

Christine Porter's fascination with floor-tile designs has inspired her to create many quilts, as explored in her book *Quilts Beneath Your Feet*. The Variable Star block was a popular choice for tiled Victorian floors and here, with its variation of inverted Flying Geese in the outer centres, it produces a secondary design of a Square Within a Square. Finished size: 66 x 66in.

April/May

Easter Monday (UK, Aus)

25 Monday

26 Tuesday

27 Wednesday

28 Thursday

29 Friday

30 Saturday

1 Sunday

MAY

M	T	W	T	F	S	S
						1
2	3	4	5	6	7	8
9	10	11	12	13	14	15
16	17	18	19	20	21	22
23	24	25	26	27	28	29
30	31					

Flowering Folds

In this pretty wall hanging, the quiltmaker Pauline Bugg has created flowers in a slightly three-dimensional design using the Folded Square technique, one of the variation methods featured in Lynne Edwards' *Cathedral Window Quilts*. Appliquéd leaves and stitched stems were added, and extra machine quilting enhanced the raised look of the design. Finished size: not known.

May

Bank Holiday (UK)

2
Monday

3
Tuesday

4
Wednesday

5
Thursday

6
Friday

7
Saturday

Mother's Day (US/Aus)

8
Sunday

MAY

M	T	W	T	F	S	S
						1
2	3	4	5	6	7	8
9	10	11	12	13	14	15
16	17	18	19	20	21	22
23	24	25	26	27	28	29
30	31					

Nine-Patch Wonder

In their book *Jell Roll Quilts*, Pam and Nicky Lintott illustrate how easy it can be to turn a jelly roll into a fabulous quilt. They found that they could make 60 Nine-Patch blocks from one roll. They alternated this versatile block with the Hourglass block to produce this soft antique-looking quilt. Finished size: 64 x 76in.

# May

9
Monday

10
Tuesday

11
Wednesday

12
Thursday

13
Friday

14
Saturday

15
Sunday

MAY

M	T	W	T	F	S	S
						1
2	3	4	5	6	7	8
9	10	11	12	13	14	15
16	17	18	19	20	21	22
23	24	25	26	27	28	29
30	31					

Time And Again

Featured in *Japanese Sashiko Inspirations*, this quilt by Susan Briscoe is simply pieced using 2in squares of vintage kimono scraps combined with contemporary batik fabric strips. The patchwork is accented with appliqué cherry blossoms made from hand-dyed cotton, and big stitch quilting. Finished size: 60 x 40in.

May

16
Monday

17
Tuesday

18
Wednesday

19
Thursday

20
Friday

21
Saturday

22
Sunday

MAY

M	T	W	T	F	S	S
						1
2	3	4	5	6	7	8
9	10	11	12	13	14	15
16	17	18	19	20	21	22
23	24	25	26	27	28	29
30	31					

Little Houses

When using layer cakes, there is a tendency to think 'big' – quiltmakers Pam and Nicky Lintott wanted to see what would happen if they thought 'small', so creating this adorable little 4½in square House block. The layer cake squares, however, are the perfect size for framing the pieced blocks, tilting the houses in different directions. For more ingenious ideas to use pre-cut fabric collections with little or no waste, see *Layer Cake, Jelly Roll and Charm Quilts*. Finished size: 58 x 58in.

May

23 Monday

24 Tuesday

25 Wednesday

26 Thursday

27 Friday

28 Saturday

29 Sunday

MAY

M	T	W	T	F	S	S
						1
2	3	4	5	6	7	8
9	10	11	12	13	14	15
16	17	18	19	20	21	22
23	24	25	26	27	28	29
30	31					

Sampler Quilt

This award-winning quilt by Susie Corke is an admirable example of using simple quilting ideas to great effect — outline and echo quilting combine with a simple motif repeated in each of the sampler blocks. This hand quilted masterpiece features in *Quilt It!*, a practical and inspirational guide to quilting options for the quiltmaker by Barbara Chainey. Finished size: not known.

May/June

Spring Bank Holiday (UK), Memorial Day (US)

30 Monday

31 Tuesday

1 Wednesday

2 Thursday

3 Friday

4 Saturday

5 Sunday

JUNE

M	T	W	T	F	S	S
		1	2	3	4	5
6	7	8	9	10	11	12
13	14	15	16	17	18	19
20	21	22	23	24	25	26
27	28	29	30			

Multicoloured Knots

A spectacular knot, formed from multicoloured bias binding, creates the centrepiece of this patchwork hanging, with borders and corner pieces formed by other knots complementing the main pattern. Gail Lawther *(More Celtic Quilting)* adapted a Celtic-inspired lace design by Leonardo da Vinci for the centrepiece, but the border and the corner knots are her own. Finished size: 53 x 53in.

June

6
Monday

7
Tuesday

8
Wednesday

9
Thursday

10
Friday

11
Saturday

12
Sunday

JUNE

M	T	W	T	F	S	S
		1	2	3	4	5
6	7	8	9	10	11	12
13	14	15	16	17	18	19
20	21	22	23	24	25	26
27	28	29	30			

Triptych Wall Hanging

The final chapter of Katharine Guerrier's *Scrap Quilt Sensation* explores how to create small 'art' quilts using fabric scraps. This three-part wall hanging incorporates techniques such as zigzags, diamonds and triangles to create the combined pattern elements, with more organic areas made by sewing randomly shaped fabric scraps together.
Finished size: each section 36 x 7¼in.

June

13
Monday

14
Tuesday

15
Wednesday

16
Thursday

17
Friday

18
Saturday

Father's Day (US/UK)

19
Sunday

JUNE						
M	T	W	T	F	S	S
		1	2	3	4	5
6	7	8	9	10	11	12
13	14	15	16	17	18	19
20	21	22	23	24	25	26
27	28	29	30			

Ohio Star Sampler

The Essential Quilter by Barbara Chainey has been described as the definitive quilting handbook. A practical sourcebook, it has creative ideas for using quilting patterns to enhance patchwork and appliqué. Each block of the small Ohio Star Sampler quilt has been quilted differently. Finished size: 34 x 47in.

June

20
Monday

21
Tuesday

22
Wednesday

23
Thursday

24
Friday

25
Saturday

26
Sunday

JUNE

M	T	W	T	F	S	S
		1	2	3	4	5
6	7	8	9	10	11	12
13	14	15	16	17	18	19
20	21	22	23	24	25	26
27	28	29	30			

Flowery Appliqué

This design from Lynne Edwards' *Making Scrap Quilts to Use It Up!* is based on her grandmother's tea set, remembered fondly from her childhood. Perfect for making a dent in her 1930s reproduction fabric stash, it combines a Nine-Patch block of assorted squares with a blanket-stitched appliquéd block. Finished size: 64 x 92in.

June/July

27
Monday

28
Tuesday

29
Wednesday

30
Thursday

1
Friday

2
Saturday

3
Sunday

JULY

M	T	W	T	F	S	S
				1	2	3
4	5	6	7	8	9	10
11	12	13	14	15	16	17
18	19	20	21	22	23	24
25	26	27	28	29	30	31

Pioneer Patches

In this version of a Friendship Star block the arms of the star have a triangle that is added in a different colour to create a Quarter-Square Triangle block. The stars then form a tessellation in strong diagonal lines in both directions. This is just one of many tessellating designs from Christine Porter's *Tessellation Quilts*. Finished size: 42 x 42in.

July

Independence Day (US)

4
Monday

5
Tuesday

6
Wednesday

7
Thursday

8
Friday

9
Saturday

10
Sunday

JULY

M	T	W	T	F	S	S
				1	2	3
4	5	6	7	8	9	10
11	12	13	14	15	16	17
18	19	20	21	22	23	24
25	26	27	28	29	30	31

Brecon Star

Mary Jenkins' Brecon Star quilt, based on an old Breconshire quilt, is typical of the many Welsh quilts made with a central medallion surrounded by randomly pieced strips in a brick-like formation. Mary and co-author Clare Claridge explore the rich history of traditional Welsh quilting in their book *Making Welsh Quilts*. Finished size: 45 x 48in.

July

11
Monday

12
Tuesday

13
Wednesday

14
Thursday

15
Friday

16
Saturday

17
Sunday

JULY

M	T	W	T	F	S	S
				1	2	3
4	5	6	7	8	9	10
11	12	13	14	15	16	17
18	19	20	21	22	23	24
25	26	27	28	29	30	31

Hokusai Wave

This beautiful wall hanging from *Easy Japanese Quilt Style* by Julia Davis and Anne Muxworthy makes wonderful use of the large Oriental fabric panels available in quilt stores. Colour elements from the panel provide a palette for the simple patchwork border. Finished size: 34 x 44in.

July

18
Monday

19
Tuesday

20
Wednesday

21
Thursday

22
Friday

23
Saturday

24
Sunday

JULY

M	T	W	T	F	S	S
				1	2	3
4	5	6	7	8	9	10
11	12	13	14	15	16	17
18	19	20	21	22	23	24
25	26	27	28	29	30	31

Tilting At Windmills

This new slant on the ever-versatile Log Cabin block features in Lynne Edwards' *Stash-Buster Quilts*. Each block is made and trimmed to an exact square. A triangular template is then used to cut off the four corners, moving them to their opposite positions before re-stitching into place. The quiltmaker, Gill Shepherd, has continued to use the tilting technique with the pieced strip borders. Finished size: not known.

July

25
Monday

26
Tuesday

27
Wednesday

28
Thursday

29
Friday

30
Saturday

31
Sunday

JULY						
M	T	W	T	F	S	S
				1	2	3
4	5	6	7	8	9	10
11	12	13	14	15	16	17
18	19	20	21	22	23	24
25	26	27	28	29	30	31

Venetian Celebration

The incredible floor tile patterns of the Basilica di San Marco (St Mark's Cathedral) in Venice date back to the 11th century. Christine Porter rose to the challenge to replicate some of the 3,000 square yards of precious 'tesserae' in her book *Quilts Beneath Your Feet*. Finished size: 104 x 104in.

August

1
Monday

2
Tuesday

3
Wednesday

4
Thursday

5
Friday

6
Saturday

7
Sunday

AUGUST

M	T	W	T	F	S	S
1	2	3	4	5	6	7
8	9	10	11	12	13	14
15	16	17	18	19	20	21
22	23	24	25	26	27	28
29	30	31				

Boxed Stars

Talented quilter Lynne Edwards contributed a chapter on Patchwork in Perspective for *The Quiltmakers*. Using a tried-and-often-tested freezer paper piecing method, Lynne has created this three-dimensional design of alternating Ohio Star and Square-in-a-Square blocks that draws you in. Finished size: not known.

August

8
Monday

9
Tuesday

10
Wednesday

11
Thursday

12
Friday

13
Saturday

14
Sunday

AUGUST

M	T	W	T	F	S	S
1	2	3	4	5	6	7
8	9	10	11	12	13	14
15	16	17	18	19	20	21
22	23	24	25	26	27	28
29	30	31				

Beach Hut Parade

Inspired by a summer holiday to Crete, quiltmaker Jenny Hutchison won second prize for this colourful quilt design which uses just one jelly roll. Her prize-winning quilt features in *Jelly Roll Inspirations* compiled by Pam and Nicky Lintott. Finished size: 48 x 64in.

August

15
Monday

16
Tuesday

17
Wednesday

18
Thursday

19
Friday

20
Saturday

21
Sunday

AUGUST

M	T	W	T	F	S	S
1	2	3	4	5	6	7
8	9	10	11	12	13	14
15	16	17	18	19	20	21
22	23	24	25	26	27	28
29	30	31				

Kimono

The kimono shape in the middle of this quilt gave Susan Briscoe the perfect background for all-over sashiko stitching. Sashiko means 'little stab', which accurately describes the simple running stitch required for this traditional technique explored fully by Susan in her book *Japanese Sashiko Inspirations*. Finished size: 39 x 27in.

August

22
Monday

23
Tuesday

24
Wednesday

25
Thursday

26
Friday

27
Saturday

28
Sunday

AUGUST

M	T	W	T	F	S	S
1	2	3	4	5	6	7
8	9	10	11	12	13	14
15	16	17	18	19	20	21
22	23	24	25	26	27	28
29	30	31				

Monoprinted Moon And Grasses

One of a sequence of four landscape-inspired hangings by Linda and Laura Kemshall developed to explore different painting techniques in their book *The Painted Quilt*. The top was strip-pieced from hand-dyed cotton and wool – a simple backdrop for the monoprinted design. Ears and stalks of barley were hand-embroidered to add an accent of colour among the vertical printed lines. Finished size: 12½ x 17in.

August/September

Summer Bank Holiday (UK)

29 Monday

30 Tuesday

31 Wednesday

1 Thursday

2 Friday

3 Saturday

Father's Day (Aus)

4 Sunday

SEPTEMBER

M	T	W	T	F	S	S
			1	2	3	4
5	6	7	8	9	10	11
12	13	14	15	16	17	18
19	20	21	22	23	24	25
26	27	28	29	30		

Snail Trail

Just one of 12 beautiful quilts featured in Katharine Guerrier's book *Scrap Quilt Sensation*, the Snail Trail is a traditional design that relies on the correct placement of contrasting fabrics for its effect. Although all the seams are straight, an illusion of curves is created, making an intriguing puzzle. Finished size: 24 x 24in.

September

Labor Day (US)

5
Monday

6
Tuesday

7
Wednesday

8
Thursday

9
Friday

10
Saturday

11
Sunday

SEPTEMBER

M	T	W	T	F	S	S
			1	2	3	4
5	6	7	8	9	10	11
12	13	14	15	16	17	18
19	20	21	22	23	24	25
26	27	28	29	30		

Tea Time

This delightful wall hanging features the tessellating T block; made by Christine Porter, it features in her book, *Tessellation Quilts*. Appliquéd T shapes and teacups have been fused on to the quilt and outlined with satin stitch, and tiny T shapes quilted above each teacup help reinforce the quilt's theme. Finished size: 32 x 32in.

September

12
Monday

13
Tuesday

14
Wednesday

15
Thursday

16
Friday

17
Saturday

18
Sunday

SEPTEMBER						
M	T	W	T	F	S	S
			1	2	3	4
5	6	7	8	9	10	11
12	13	14	15	16	17	18
19	20	21	22	23	24	25
26	27	28	29	30		

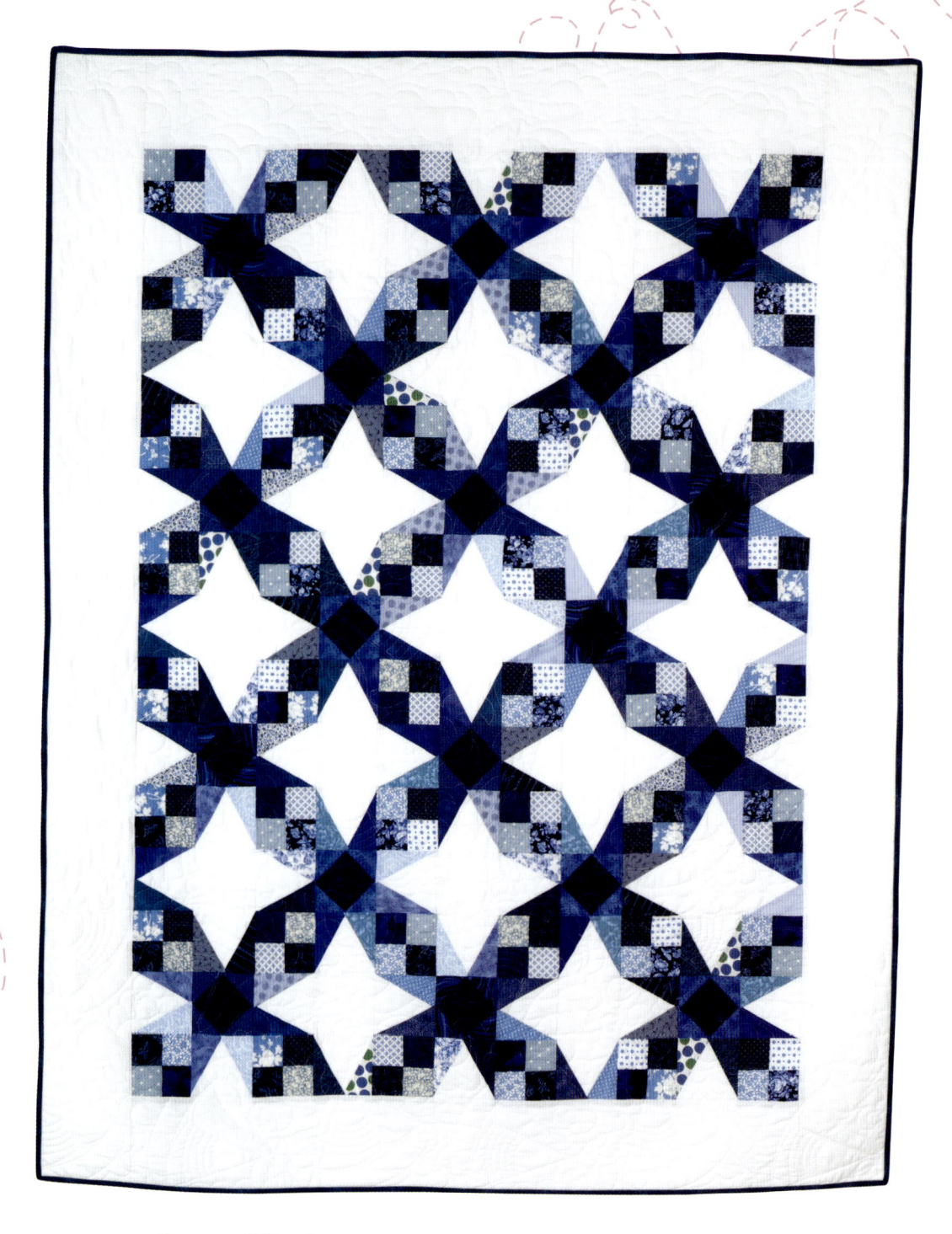

Stormy Weather

This stunning quilt (featured in *Layer Cake, Jelly Roll and Charm Quilts* by Pam and Nicky Lintott) is made from just one blue jelly roll combined with white on white fabric for a crisp, fresh look. This design has only straight lines to sew, yet gives the appearance of curves. Ingenious! Finished size: 56 x 72in.

September

19
Monday

20
Tuesday

21
Wednesday

22
Thursday

23
Friday

24
Saturday

25
Sunday

SEPTEMBER

M	T	W	T	F	S	S
			1	2	3	4
5	6	7	8	9	10	11
12	13	14	15	16	17	18
19	20	21	22	23	24	25
26	27	28	29	30		

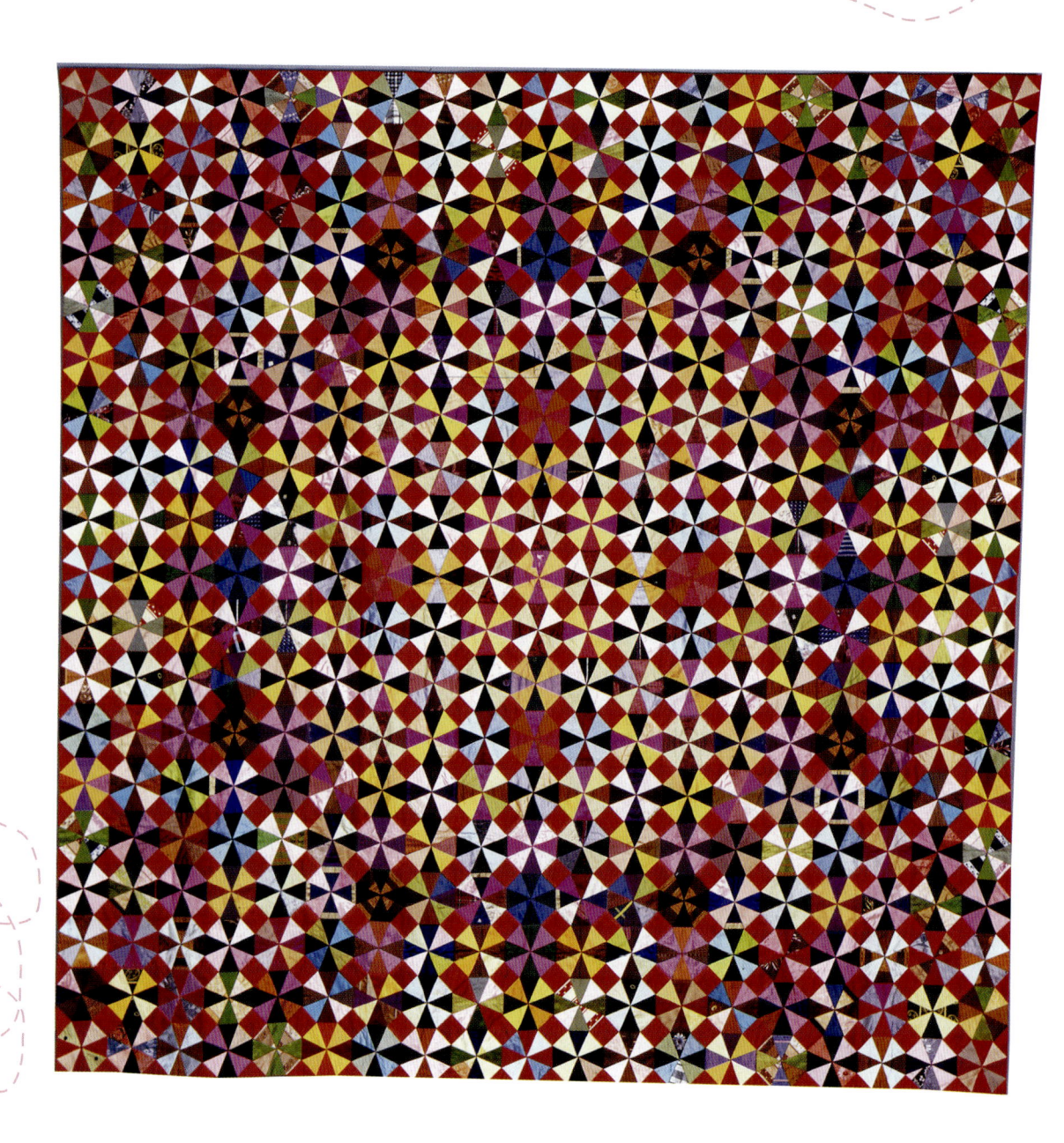

Kaleidoscope Pattern

This kaleidoscope pattern mosaic quilt, made in silk by Elizabeth Watson of Cumbria in the late 19th century, forms part of the Heritage Collection. More examples of this amazing body of work can be seen in *The Quilters' Guild Collection*. Finished size: 85 x 86½in.

September/October

26
Monday

27
Tuesday

28
Wednesday

29
Thursday

30
Friday

1
Saturday

2
Sunday

OCTOBER

M	T	W	T	F	S	S
					1	2
3	4	5	6	7	8	9
10	11	12	13	14	15	16
17	18	19	20	21	22	23
24	25	26	27	28	29	30
31						

Amish Lilies

In *Quilt It!*, Barbara Chainey sets out to answer the 'how do I quilt it?' questions she has heard time and time again in the classes and quilting groups she has run over the years. Take your cue from the quilt itself, she advises: for example, this quilt made by Sandie Lush features the curving lines of a lily quilting motif in contrast to the straight edges of the stylized lily pieced blocks. Finished size: not known.

October

3
Monday

4
Tuesday

5
Wednesday

6
Thursday

7
Friday

8
Saturday

9
Sunday

OCTOBER

M	T	W	T	F	S	S
					1	2
3	4	5	6	7	8	9
10	11	12	13	14	15	16
17	18	19	20	21	22	23
24	25	26	27	28	29	30
31						

Birthday Gift

This quilt by Annie Harris won third place in the Jelly Roll Challenge, an international competition first held in 2009 for great quilt designs made from just one jelly roll. The quilt was named for the block design, which Annie decided resembled the top of a gift-wrapped box. All the winning quilts are published in a book, *Jelly Roll Inspirations*, compiled by Pam and Nicky Lintott. Finished size: 60 x 60in.

October

Columbus Day (US)

10
Monday

11
Tuesday

12
Wednesday

13
Thursday

14
Friday

15
Saturday

16
Sunday

OCTOBER

M	T	W	T	F	S	S
					1	2
3	4	5	6	7	8	9
10	11	12	13	14	15	16
17	18	19	20	21	22	23
24	25	26	27	28	29	30
31						

In The Red

In *Stash-Buster Quilts* Lynne Edwards continues her campaign to help the quilter reduce their fabric collection by offering time-saving designs for fabric leftovers. In Sheila Piper's interpretation of the tessellating maple leaf design she has used just one red fabric as the alternating leaf shape, which contrasts wonderfully with the lighter black and white leaves. Finished size: 64 x 88in.

October

17
Monday

18
Tuesday

19
Wednesday

20
Thursday

21
Friday

22
Saturday

23
Sunday

OCTOBER

M	T	W	T	F	S	S
					1	2
3	4	5	6	7	8	9
10	11	12	13	14	15	16
17	18	19	20	21	22	23
24	25	26	27	28	29	30
31						

Zen – Garden From The Tea House

Susan Briscoe (*Japanese Sashiko Inspirations*) was inspired by a Kyoto-style tearoom to create this stunning quilt. An appliquéd tea bowl awaits the guest, and big stitch quilting suggests the raked gravel garden seen through the low doorway. Finished size: 37 x 25in.

October

24
Monday

25
Tuesday

26
Wednesday

27
Thursday

28
Friday

29
Saturday

30
Sunday

| OCTOBER |||||||
M	T	W	T	F	S	S
					1	2
3	4	5	6	7	8	9
10	11	12	13	14	15	16
17	18	19	20	21	22	23
24	25	26	27	28	29	30
31						

Debbie In De Nile

Quiltmaker Barbara Chainey decided to take action against her five-year collection of fat quarter selections, and *Fast Quilts from Fat Quarters* was the happy result. This book is full of quilt designs that have been created following the cutting plan developed by Barbara for cutting a whole stack of quarters into useable shapes in one go. Debbie Fetch designed this lively sampler-style quilt, with its jaunty twist-and-turn setting. Finished size: 38 x 48in.

October/November

Halloween

31 Monday

1 Tuesday

2 Wednesday

3 Thursday

4 Friday

5 Saturday

6 Sunday

			NOVEMBER			
M	T	W	T	F	S	S
	1	2	3	4	5	6
7	8	9	10	11	12	13
14	15	16	17	18	19	20
21	22	23	24	25	26	27
28	29	30				

Snowball Nine-Patch

This quilt, made by Collie Parker and featured in *Making Scrap Quilts to Use It Up!*, alternates a Snowball block with a Nine-Patch. It is a real scrap quilt, using as many fabrics as possible with just one calming fabric used as the main shape in the centre of each Snowball block. Finished size: 88 x 74½in.

November

7
Monday

8
Tuesday

9
Wednesday

10
Thursday

Veterans Day (US), Remembrance Day (Aus)

11
Friday

12
Saturday

13
Sunday

NOVEMBER

M	T	W	T	F	S	S
	1	2	3	4	5	6
7	8	9	10	11	12	13
14	15	16	17	18	19	20
21	22	23	24	25	26	27
28	29	30				

Amish Spiral

In her book *More Celtic Quilting* Gail Lawther explores the popular motifs of Celtic art – a rich source of inspiration for quilters. Here a variety of flowing spiral patterns have been big-stitch quilted on to a pieced background inspired by the traditional colours and shapes of Amish quilts, a magnificent combination of two great traditions on one piece of work.
Finished size: 40 x 40in.

November

14
Monday

15
Tuesday

16
Wednesday

17
Thursday

18
Friday

19
Saturday

20
Sunday

NOVEMBER						
M	T	W	T	F	S	S
	1	2	3	4	5	6
7	8	9	10	11	12	13
14	15	16	17	18	19	20
21	22	23	24	25	26	27
28	29	30				

Country-Style Welcome

This quilt by Australian-based quiltmaker Lynette Anderson-O'Rourke featured in *The Quiltmakers*, and it combines primitive folk art with a traditional country look. A variety of techniques are included such as piecing and appliqué, blanket stitch appliqué, bias strips (flower stems), yoyos (flower centres) and a small amount of embroidery.
Finished size: 45½ x 52in.

November

21
Monday

22
Tuesday

23
Wednesday

Thanksgiving (US)   **24**
Thursday

25
Friday

26
Saturday

27
Sunday

NOVEMBER

M	T	W	T	F	S	S
	1	2	3	4	5	6
7	8	9	10	11	12	13
14	15	16	17	18	19	20
21	22	23	24	25	26	27
28	29	30				

Winter Solstice

This gorgeous seasonal wall hanging, with its striking black, cream and gold colouring, is featured in Lynne Edwards' *Cathedral Window Quilts*. Lynne has edged a complex centre of classic Cathedral Windows with a border of Twisted Windows. Finished size: 27 x 27in.

November/December

28 Monday

29 Tuesday

30 Wednesday

1 Thursday

2 Friday

3 Saturday

4 Sunday

DECEMBER

M	T	W	T	F	S	S
			1	2	3	4
5	6	7	8	9	10	11
12	13	14	15	16	17	18
19	20	21	22	23	24	25
26	27	28	29	30	31	

Sashiko Sampler

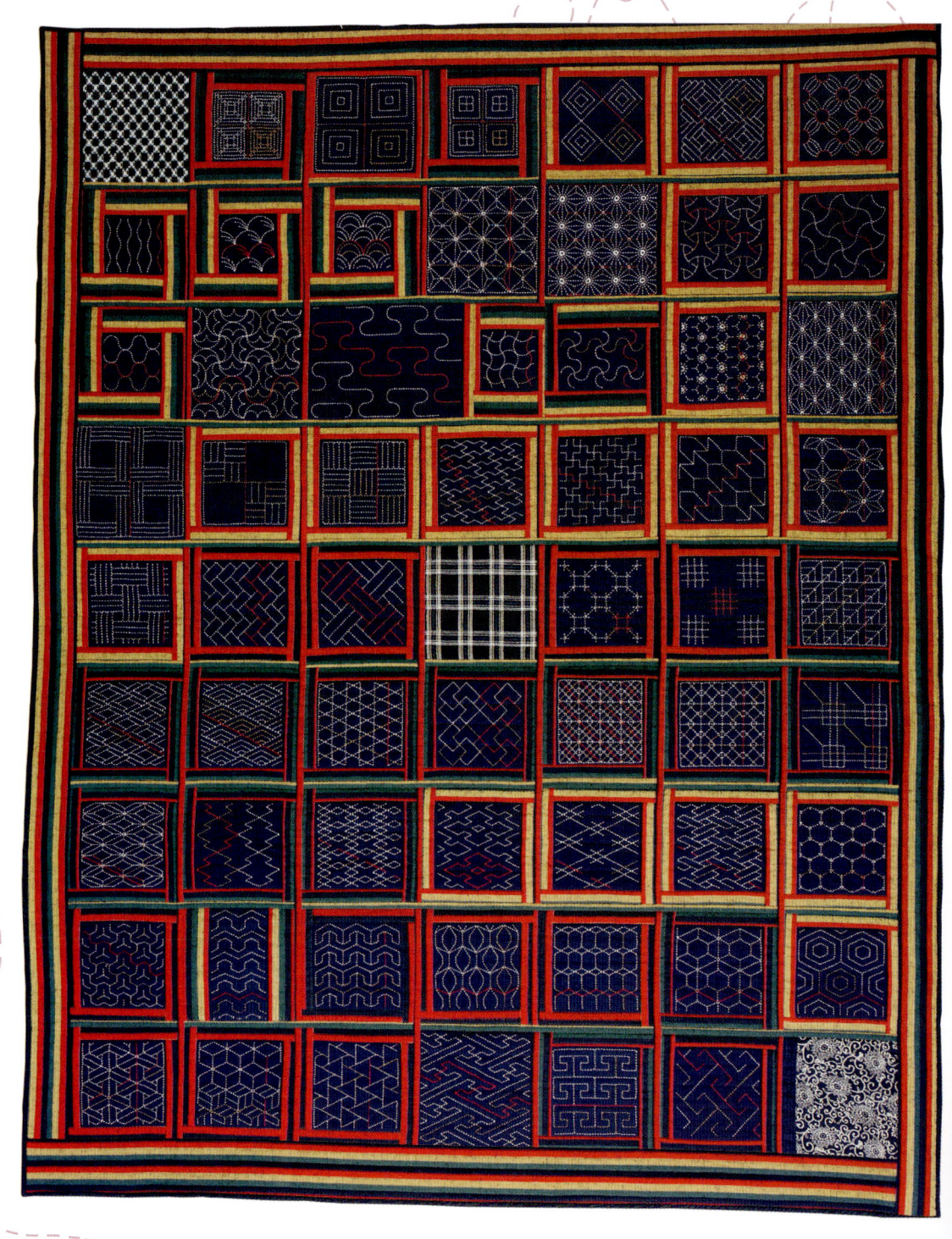

This sashiko sampler quilt by Susan Briscoe features 60 different samples of *mayōzashi* (pattern sashiko) samples bordered with striped *tsumugi* cotton. These represent just over half of the sashi pattern library featured in her book *The Ultimate Sashiko Sourcebook*. Finished size: 67 x 84in.

December

5
Monday

6
Tuesday

7
Wednesday

8
Thursday

9
Friday

10
Saturday

11
Sunday

DECEMBER

M	T	W	T	F	S	S
			1	2	3	4
5	6	7	8	9	10	11
12	13	14	15	16	17	18
19	20	21	22	23	24	25
26	27	28	29	30	31	

Green Beans And Red Berries

This jewel of a Christmas quilt using jelly roll fabrics featured in Pam and Nicky Lintott's *Jelly Roll Quilts*. It uses Four-Patch, Nine-Patch and Flying Geese units to form a striking design. Finished size: 72 x 72in.

December

12
Monday

13
Tuesday

14
Wednesday

15
Thursday

16
Friday

17
Saturday

18
Sunday

DECEMBER

M	T	W	T	F	S	S
			1	2	3	4
5	6	7	8	9	10	11
12	13	14	15	16	17	18
19	20	21	22	23	24	25
26	27	28	29	30	31	

Sew A Row Of Christmas

This lovely Christmas quilt from Mandy Shaw's *Quilt Yourself Gorgeous* has it all – appliqué, foundation piecing, stitch and flip, and fast piecing. It may look complicated, but it is actually quite straightforward as each of the five bands is worked separately, and the buttons and embellishments are sewn on at the very end. Finished size: 37½ x 44½in.

December

19
Monday

20
Tuesday

21
Wednesday

22
Thursday

23
Friday

24
Saturday

Christmas Day

25
Sunday

M	T	W	T	F	S	S
			1	2	3	4
5	6	7	8	9	10	11
12	13	14	15	16	17	18
19	20	21	22	23	24	25
26	27	28	29	30	31	

DECEMBER

Star Bright

This stunning quilt by Marianne Bennett featured in Lynne Edwards' *Stash-Buster Quilts*. Two blocks, both based on 3in finished squares – the simple Nine-Patch and a Star Nine-Patch, where the star 'floats' on a background fabric – complement each other perfectly. Finished size: 97 x 97in.

December/January

Boxing Day (UK, Aus)

26 Monday

Bank Holiday (UK, Aus)

27 Tuesday

28 Wednesday

29 Thursday

30 Friday

31 Saturday

New Year's Day

1 Sunday

DECEMBER

M	T	W	T	F	S	S
			1	2	3	4
5	6	7	8	9	10	11
12	13	14	15	16	17	18
19	20	21	22	23	24	25
26	27	28	29	30	31	

Useful Information

It is hoped that the quilt photographs featured in this diary have inspired you to take your own quilt skills further. Wherever you are located, there are bound to be opportunities for you to see other quilters' work and to share your love of this amazing textile art. Use the following information to help you find out what is going on near you.

UK

Organizations

The Quilters' Guild of the British Isles is an independent registered educational charity with over 7,000 members. www.quiltersguild.org.uk

Exhibitions

The Festival of Quilts
Organized by Creative Exhibitions Ltd with the support of the Quilters Guild of the British Isles, this is the largest quilt show in Europe with over 27,000 visitors each year. A four-day show held in August at the National Exhibition Centre, Birmingham, it has over 1,000 competition quilts on display, as well as galleries from leading international quilt artists and groups. There are over 250 exhibitors selling specialist patchwork and quilting supplies, plus hundreds of masterclasses, workshops and lectures.
www.twistedthread.com

Quilts UK
The organizers of this exhibition, Grosvenor Shows Ltd, hold several patchwork and quilting exhibitions nationally each year. The largest of these is Quilts UK held in May at the Three Counties Showground in the beautiful Malvern Hills in Worcestershire. The longest established show in the UK, it attracts over 9,000 visitors annually. It is an open competitive show with over 400 quilts on display and 150 trade stands.
www.grosvenorexhibitions.co.uk

The National Quilt Championships
An open competitive quilt show held at Sandown Park in June attracting over 5,000 visitors. Over 400 quilts are on display, including features from well-known artists from the UK and overseas, incorporating a mix of traditional and contemporary quilts.
www.grosvenorexhibitions.co.uk

Spring and Autumn Quilt Festivals
A number of smaller, local quilt shows are also organized by Grosvenor Shows Ltd. Locations include: Ardingly, Exeter, Chilford, Edinburgh, and Malvern.
www.grosvenorexhibitions.co.uk

Quiltfest
Quiltfest's aim is to showcase the cutting edge of textile design and making, and to enable quiltmakers in Wales and the Northwest of England to see work that may not normally be exhibited in the region. It is an annual show held in February at Llangollen Museum and Art Gallery.
www.quiltfest.org.uk

USA

Organizations

American Quilter's Society (AQS)
The aim of the AQS is to provide a forum for quilters of all skill levels to expand their horizons in quiltmaking, design, self-expression and quilt collecting. It publishes books and magazines, has product offers, and runs quilt shows and contests, workshops and other activities.
www.americanquilter.com

The International Quilting Association (IQA)
The IQA is a non-profit organization dedicated to the preservation of the art of quilting, the attainment of public recognition for quilting as an art form, and the advancement of the state of the art throughout the world. Founded in 1979, it supports many quilting projects and activities, and organizes two annual Judged Shows of members' work exhibited at the International Quilt Markets and Festivals held throughout the year.
www.quilts.com

Exhibitions

American Quilter's Society Quilt Shows
The AQS organizes a number of quilt shows annually and in 2011 these will be held in Lancaster, Pennsylvania (March), Paducah, Kentucky (April), Knoxville, Tennessee (July), and Des Moines, Iowa (September).
www.americanquilter.com

The International Quilting Association Quilt Shows
Quilts, Inc., the IQA's exhibiton arm, holds three consumer shows (Quilt Festival) and two trade shows (Quilt Market) annually.
www.quilts.com

Sisters Quilt Show
This is the largest outdoor quilt show in the world with over 12,500 attendees and is held on the second Saturday of July in Sisters, Oregon.
www.SistersOutdoorQuiltShow.org

The Mancuso Quilt Shows
Mancuso Show Management, run by brothers David and Peter Mancuso, promotes six major national and international quilting and textile arts festivals held across the USA.
www.quiltfest.com

CANADA
Organizations

Canadian Quilters' Association
Formed in 1981, the aims and objectives of the Canadian Quilters' Association are: to promote a greater understanding, appreciation, and knowledge of the art, techniques, and heritage of patchwork, appliqué, and quilting; to promote the highest standards of workmanship and design in both traditional and innovative work; and to foster cooperation and sharing among quiltmakers. There are a number of Canadian Quilters' Association sponsored events including the National Juried Show (NJS), Canada's most prestigious quilt show.
www.canadianquilter.com

AUSTRALIA
Organizations

The Quilters' Guild of NSW
A Sydney-based organization which aims to promote the art and craft of patchwork and quilting. Membership is open to anyone with an interest in the craft, from the beginner to the professional, and it has over 1,000 members.
www.quiltersguildnsw.com

Quilters' Guild of South Australia
This organization has over 500 individual guild members with over 100 city and country groups now affiliated with the guild.
www.saquilters.org.au

Exhibitions

Australia's No.1 Craft and Quilt Fairs
Expertise Events run several craft and quilting fairs in Australia (Perth, Sydney, Hobart, Melbourne, Canberra, Brisbane, Adelaide and Newcastle) and New Zealand (Christchurch, Hamilton).
www.craftfair.com.au

The Australasian Quilt Convention (AQC)
Held in Melbourne, this is Australia's largest annual quilt-dedicated event, incorporating classes and lectures with highly skilled tutors, much-anticipated social events, a shopping market plus exhibitor workshops and exclusive quilt displays. It brings together thousands of quilters from all over Australia and around the world.
www.aqc.com.au

NEW ZEALAND
Organizations

National Association of New Zealand Quilters (NANZQ)
The National Association of New Zealand Quilters' principle objective is to promote and lead the development of patchwork, quilting and textile artists within New Zealand.
www.nanzq.org.nz

Exhibitions

National Patchwork and Quilting Symposium
Held annually in Queenstown, this five-day event is the largest, most prestigious event for New Zealand quilters. Up to 1,500 New Zealand and overseas participants are involved, attending a wide range of classes and workshops, lectures, merchants' markets and exhibitions, among other activities. There are over 50 classes a day, tutored by well-known overseas and national tutors.
www.remarkablesymposium2011.org.nz

More About The Quilts

The quilts included in the *Quilter's Desk Diary 2011* have all been selected from the great range of patchwork and quilting books published by David & Charles. If you would like to find out more about any of the quilt designs featured, why not treat yourself to a few of these great books. For more information about these and other high quality craft books from David & Charles visit: www.rucraft.co.uk

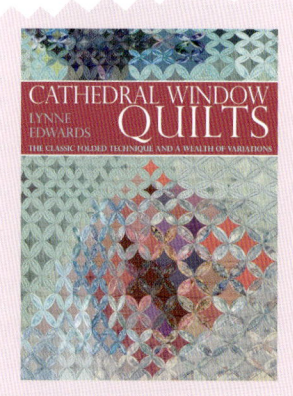

Cathedral Window Quilts
Lynne Edwards

ISBN-13: 978-0-7153-2713-5

Explore classic techniques using fabulous fabrics to create over 25 flamboyantly folded projects, ranging from heirloom quilts and striking wall hangings to colourful, quick-to-make cushions, bags and pincushions.

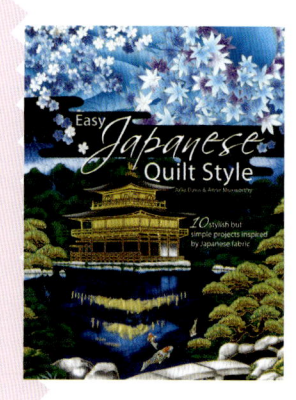

Easy Japanese Quilt Style
Julia Davis & Anne Muxworthy

ISBN-13: 978-0-7153-2862-0

The perfect book for quilters of all abilities who want to introduce Japanese style into their homes with ingenious quick-to-stitch projects, ranging from bags to wall hangings.

The Essential Quilter
Barbara Chainey

ISBN-13: 978-0-7153-0569-7

The Essential Quilter presents history and tradition, design sources and ideas, practical instruction and trace-off motifs. Stylishly illustrated throughout, this is the must-have book for quilters of all abilities.

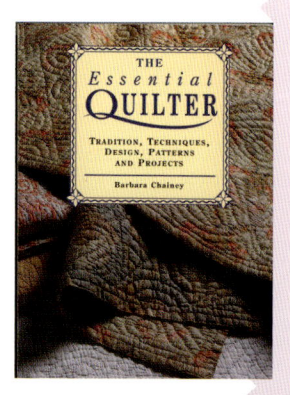

Fast Quilts from Fat Quarters
Barbara Chainey

ISBN-13: 978-0-7153-2462-2

With its easy-to-use cutting plan, learn how to take fat quarters and quickly turn them into unique quilts of all shapes and sizes. Features 15 step-by-step projects from small wall hangings to full-size bed quilts.

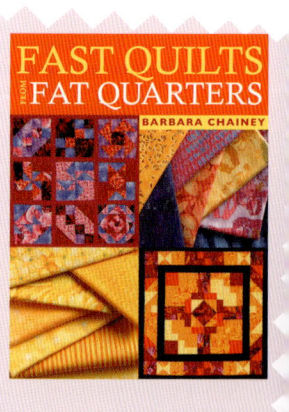

Japanese Sashiko Inspirations
Susan Briscoe

ISBN-13: 978-0-7153-2641-4

Discover sashiko, the Japanese method of decorative stitching to create striking patterns on fabric with lines of simple running stitch. Bring a touch of the Orient to your home with over 25 projects to choose from.

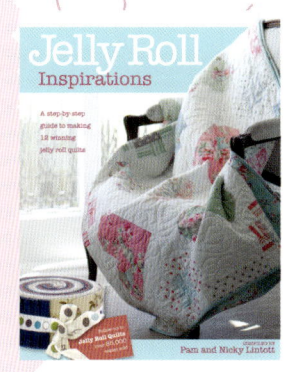

Jelly Roll Inspirations
Pam & Nicky Lintott

ISBN-13: 978-0-7153-3311-2

The aim of the Jelly Roll Challenge competition was to find the best and most creative use of just one jelly roll. Gathered here are the 12 fabulous winning entries, with step-by-step instructions and a colour variation on each.

Jelly Roll Quilts
Pam & Nicky Lintott

ISBN-13: 978-0-7153-2863-7

Jelly Roll Quilts was the first book on the market to show the best ways to use these desirable and labour-saving fabric packs consisting of 2½ inch strips of colour co-ordinated fabric. There are 17 designs, each of which can be made from just one roll.

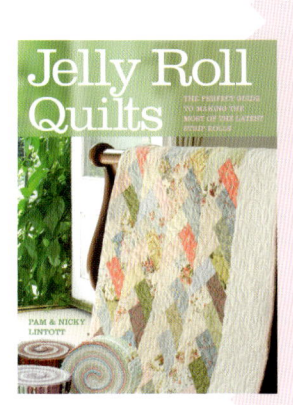

Layer Cake, Jelly Roll and Charm Quilts
Pam & Nicky Lintott

ISBN-13: 978-0-7153-3208-5

Seventeen beautiful projects, from lap quilts to bed quilts, show you how to get the most from irresistible pre-cut fabric bundles.

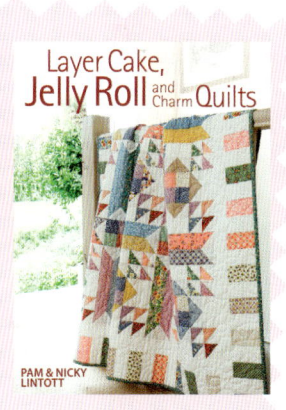

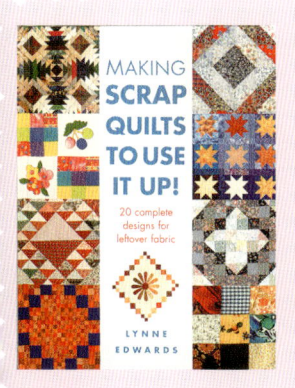

Making Scrap Quilts to Use It Up!
Lynne Edwards

ISBN-13: 978-0-7153-1412-8

Almost half the fabrics bought are on impulse without a use in mind. Add to this project leftovers and you have an ever-growing hoard of material to use up. This book has inspirational ways of making quilts with fabrics from your stash.

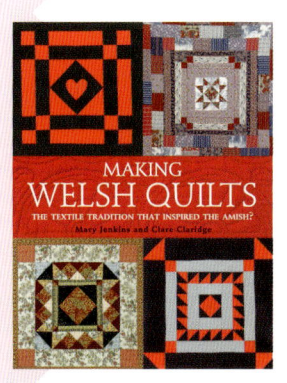

Making Welsh Quilts
Mary Jenkins & Clare Claridge

ISBN-13: 978-0-7153-2996-2

This book explores the fascinating history of Welsh quilting and features 10 sumptuous projects for you to make in the traditional style, using strikingly simple patchwork designs and decorative quilting patterns.

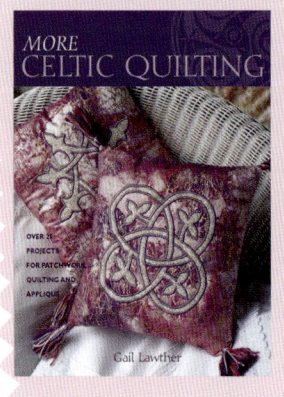

More Celtic Quilting
Gail Lawther

ISBN-13: 978-0-7153-1693-1

A collection of 25 patchwork, quilting and appliqué projects exploring the four most popular areas of Celtic design: knotwork; spirals; key, fret and carpet patterns; plants and animals.

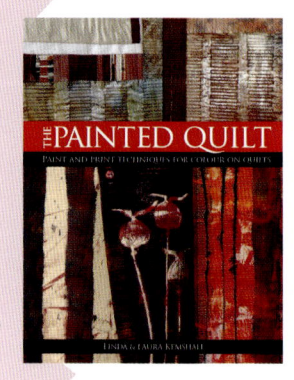

The Painted Quilt
Linda & Laura Kemshall

ISBN-13: 978-0-7153-2450-9

This inspirational book demystifies the process of colouring cloth by various means including fabric paints, pastels, dyes, bleaches and transfers. Simple techniques are combined to produce complex textile surfaces, all easily explained step-by-step.

The Quilter's Guild Collection
Editor: Bridget Long

ISBN-13: 978-0-7153-2668-8

The Quilter's Guild Heritage Collection is the largest collection of patchwork and quilting in the UK, dating back as far as the 18th century. Twelve contemporary quiltmakers each take inspiration from a heritage piece to make a project for today.

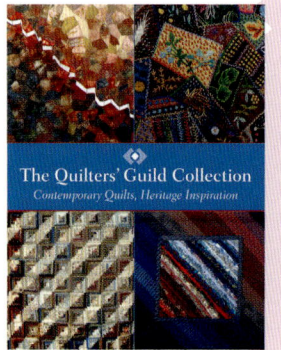

Quilt It!
Barbara Chainey

ISBN-13: 978-0-7153-1220-0

A practical and inspirational guide to quilting options for patchwork and appliqué. This is the essential resource for hand and machine quilters of all skill levels.

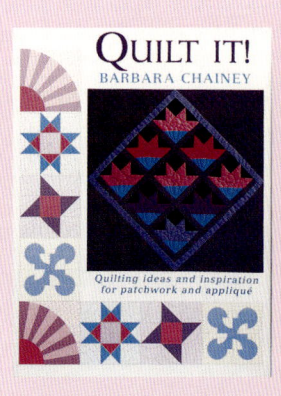

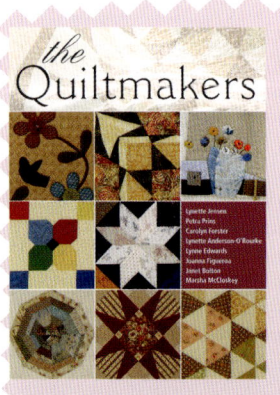

The Quiltmakers
Consultant Editor: Pam Lintott

ISBN-13: 978-0-7153-3173-6

A unique opportunity to take eight masterclasses from some of the very best quilters in the world, without ever leaving home. Topics include creating perspective, perfect piecing, and inspired fabric collage.

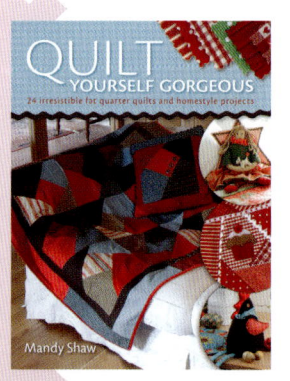

Quilt Yourself Gorgeous
Mandy Shaw

ISBN-13: 978-0-7153-2830-9

Mandy has a fresh approach to quilting with an emphasis on fun, fast results and fabulous quilts. She includes 20 brilliant projects that have plenty of wow factor, but won't take a lifetime to complete.

Quilts Beneath Your Feet
Christine Porter

ISBN-13: 978-0-7153-3293-1

An exciting collection of 10 original pieced patchwork quilt designs together with variation ideas, all inspired by traditional floor tiles from churches, cathedrals and historic buildings around the world.

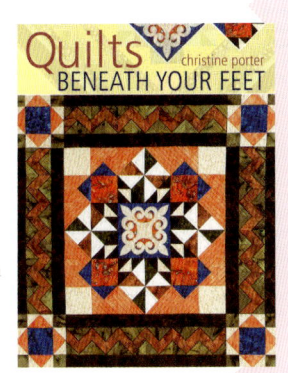

Scrap Quilt Sensation
Katharine Guerrier

ISBN-13: 978-0-7153-2452-3

A sumptuous collection of scrap quilts with a contemporary twist on traditional designs. Twelve step-by-step projects, with in-depth advice on selecting the right fabrics from your stash and how to combine them for best effect.

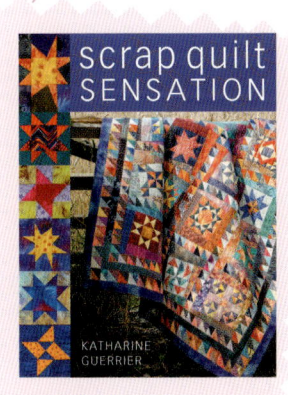

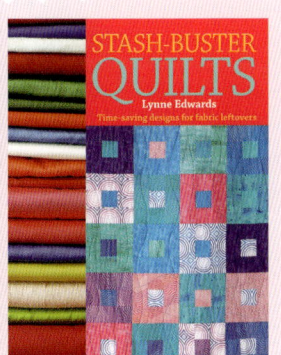

Stash-Buster Quilts
Lynne Edwards

ISBN-13: 978-0-7153-2463-2

Lynne Edwards continues her campaign to help you reduce your fabric collection leaving you free to buy more. Twenty scrap quilts are described, as well as a selection of smaller projects, from bags to soft toys, to ensure every last scrap is used up.

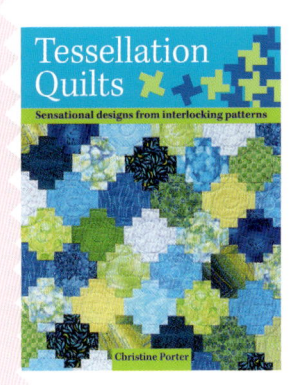

Tessellation Quilts
Christine Porter

ISBN-13: 978-0-7153-1941-3

Discover how you can translate simple interlocking patterns into stunning pieced patchwork designs. Nine tessellating block designs are explored in detail, with over 45 quilts illustrating how the blocks can be used in very different ways.

The Ultimate Sashiko Sourcebook
Susan Briscoe

ISBN-13: 978-0-7153-1847-0

Sashiko means 'little stab', which accurately describes the simple running stitch required for this traditional technique. Featured are over 100 stunning decorative sashiko patterns alongside 10 easy-to-make projects.

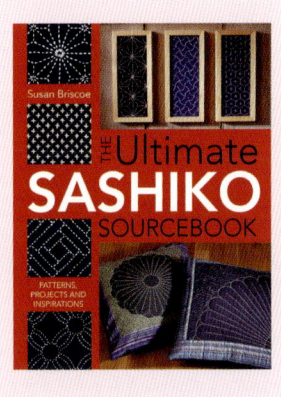

More About The Quiltmakers

The quilt designs featured in *The Quilter's Desk Diary 2011* showcase the talents of some of the world's most respected and creative quiltmakers. The names of those whose work is included are listed below.

Helen Allinson is the winner of the Jelly Roll Challenge 2009. Her quilt, Be My Valentine, featuring a soft and romantic design, appears both as a project and on the front cover of *Jelly Roll Inspirations*.

Lynette Anderson-O'Rourke was born in Dorset, England and moved to Australia in 1990 where she founded The Patchwork Angel store in 1997. Lynette is now focussed full time on designing her extensive pattern range, as well as fabrics for Henry Glass & Co. She lives in Pacific Paradise, Queensland.
www.lynetteandersondesigns.typepad.com

Susan Briscoe was introduced to sashiko while teaching English in Japan. Susan's sashiko designs have been published in *Popular Patchwork*, *British Patchwork & Quilting* and *Fabrications*, and her books include *21 Terrific Patchwork Bags*, *21 Sensational Patchwork Bags* and *Fabulous Fat Quarter Bags*. She lives in Wrexham.
www.susanbriscoe.co.uk

Barbara Chainey maintains a busy national and international teaching schedule including the prestigious International Quilt Festival at Houston, as well as offering regular classes in the UK. Over 150 of her quality designs have been translated into stencils. Her best-selling title, *The Essential Quilter*, is widely considered to be the definitive quilting handbook. She lives near Leek, Staffordshire.
www.chrisandbarbara.co.uk

Clare Claridge is a world expert on Welsh quilting patterns, and she has co-authored a book about this passion. *Making Welsh Quilts* encourages quilters to develop their own designs to take the craft into the 21st century. Clare lives in Quakers' Yard, South Wales, once a stronghold of traditional Welsh quilting in the heart of the valleys.
www.welshquilts.co.uk

Julia Davis runs the Step By Step Patchwork Centre together with Anne Muxworthy. This is a busy quilt shop in South Molton, Devon, holding regular workshops and hosting visiting quilting groups. They specialize in Japanese fabrics, importing the Kona Bay range from the US, and offer several kits that make great use of them.
www.stepbystep-quilts.co.uk

Lynne Edwards specializes in sampler quilts and the cathedral window technique. She has been the recipient of many prestigious awards including the Jewel Pearce Patterson Scholarship for International Quilt Teachers and the Amy Emms Memorial Trophy. In 2008 she was awarded an MBE for services to Arts and Crafts. Lynne lives near Ipswich, Suffolk.

Carolyn Forster studied textiles at Bath and has a City & Guilds in Patchwork and Quilting. She teaches widely and has been featured in *Fabrications*, *Popular Patchwork* and *British Patchwork & Quilting*. Carolyn's quilts have appeared on television, both in the UK and the US. She lives in Tunbridge Wells, Kent.
www.carolynforster.co.uk

Katharine Guerrier is the author of numerous books including *Quilting from Start to Finish* and *Scrap Quilt Sensation*. She also contributes regularly to several quilting magazines with articles, projects and reviews. Katharine lives in Worcester.
www.katharineguerrier.com

Annie Harris is the designer and creator of the beautiful Birthday Gift quilt which took third prize in the 2009 Jelly Roll Challenge. Annie's quilt now features as a project in Pam & Nicky Lintott's *Jelly Roll Inspirations*.

Jenny Hutchison won second prize in the 2009 Jelly Roll Challenge. Her colourful Beach Hut Parade quilt now features as a project in *Jelly Roll Inspirations*.

Mary Jenkins teaches textiles in Adult Education and is a collector of Welsh quilts and samplers. Mary is an experienced author and has written several books including co-authoring *Making Welsh Quilts*. Mary lives in Cardiff, Wales.
www.welshquilts.co.uk

Laura Kemshall works alongside her mother Linda Kemshall to offer a range of City & Guilds creative courses through their fully accredited online centre. She also designs and produces an exclusive range of products available through her online DesignMatters Store. Laura lives in Wolverhampton, West Midlands.
www.lindakemshall.com/Laura

Linda Kemshall and her daughter Laura are renowned for their innovative approach to textiles as well as their online teaching courses. They have exhibited at many prestigious events all over the world to critical acclaim, and won several major awards for innovative design, use of colour and machine appliqué and quilting. Linda lives in Wolverhampton, West Midlands.
www.lindakemshall.com

Gail Lawther, an award-winning quilter, is well known as a teacher and demonstrator. She is the author of many books, including *Fun & Fabulous Patchwork & Appliqué* and *Celtic Quilting*. She has won numerous awards at national quilt festivals. Gail lives near Lancing, West Sussex.
www.gail-quilts-plus.co.uk

Nicky Lintott runs The Quilt Room in Dorking, Surrey, together with her mother Pam Lintott. An excellent quilter in her own right, Nicky's focus is on developing the long arm quilting business.
www.quiltroom.co.uk

Pam Lintott part-owns The Quilt Room with her daughter Nicky. Her first book, *The Quilt Room*, was a compilation of work from the very best patchworkers. Pam has also written several books with Nicky including the phenomenally successful *Jelly Roll Quilts*. Pam lives near Liskeard, Cornwall.
www.quiltroom.co.uk

Marsha McCloskey was originally a graphic artist but in 1969 she turned from printmaking to quiltmaking. She now teaches, specializing in Feathered Star designs. Marsha has written and co-authored over 25 books on quiltmaking, including *Marsha McCloskey's Block Party*. She also runs Feathered Star Productions, Inc., an online resource for her materials and books. She lives in Eugene, Oregon.
www.marshamccloskey.com

Anne Muxworthy runs the Step by Step Patchwork Centre in South Molton, Devon, alongside Julia Davis. They regularly display their Japanese fabrics at shows where they enjoy sharing their knowledge on how to use them creatively by running workshops and classes.
www.stepbystep-quilts.co.uk

Christine Porter teaches, lectures and judges in the US, Canada, Europe and the Middle East. She is the British coordinator for the World Quilt and Textile competition and her quilts have won many awards internationally. Co-editor of *British Patchwork & Quilting* for several years, she is now a regular contributor of articles to quilting magazines. Christine lives near Bristol.
www.christineporterquilts.com

Petra Prins has had an interest in antique reproduction fabrics since she was very young. She opened her shop in Zutphen in 2000. She offers a range of beautiful quilt packages and creative courses through her website. Petra lives in Amsterdam, The Netherlands.
www.petraprinspatchwork.nl

Jo Rednall started making quilts at an evening class after seeing a log cabin quilt at a church fair. Once retired from a career in computing, she successfully completed a City & Guilds Patchwork and Quilting course. Her award-winning red and white quilt featured in *The Quilters' Guild Collection*.

Mandy Shaw runs Dandelion Designs, a craft design and kit company. Her work has featured on several TV programmes including *Kirstie's Homemade Christmas* (Channel 4), and she has written for *Popular Patchwork*, *Homespun* and *Fabrications* magazines. She teaches all over the country and her fast, trendy, no-fuss approach to patchwork makes her classes consistently popular. She lives near Hailsham, East Sussex.
www.dandeliondesigns.co.uk

The Quilters' Guild of the British Isles is an independent registered educational charity with over 7,000 members, which is dedicated to preserving the heritage and craft of quilting and patchwork in the UK. The Guild has its Head Office and Museum at St Anthony's Hall, Peasholme Green in York, where many of the 700 items in its quilt collection are on permanent display. The Quilters' Guild is divided into 18 regions throughout the UK. Each regional committee organizes regional days and area days, several times a year, with speakers, competitions and events that are supported by local traders. Each region has a newsletter that advises members of local events and items of interest.
www.quiltersguild.org.uk

www.kalquilts.com

KALEIDOSCOPE

• BOOKS • FABRIC • WADDING •

Sponsors of Viewers' Choice Festival of Quilts, NEC

www.candh.co.uk

C & H

C & H Fabrics stores located at:

BRIGHTON
179 Western Road, Brighton, Sussex BN1 2BA.
Tel: (01273) 321959 Fax: (01273) 736224

GUILDFORD
6a Tungsgate Square, Guildford, Surrey GU1 3QZ.
Tel: (01483) 301380 Fax: (01483) 301389

CHICHESTER
33/34 North Street, Chichester, West Sussex PO19 1LX.
Tel: (01243) 783300 Fax: (01243) 788555

TUNBRIDGE WELLS
113/115 Mount Pleasant, Tunbridge Wells, Kent TN1 1QS.
Tel: (01892) 522618 Fax: (01892) 517404

WINCHESTER
8 High Street, Winchester, Hants SO23 9JX.
Tel: (01962) 843355 Fax: (01962) 849928

EASTBOURNE
82/86 Terminus Road, Eastbourne, East Sussex BN21 3LX.
Tel: (01323) 410428 Fax: (01323) 416029

CANTERBURY
2 St. George's Street, Canterbury, Kent CT1 2SR.
Tel: (01227) 459760 Fax: (01227) 781837

MAIDSTONE
68 Week Street, Maidstone, Kent ME14 1RJ.
Tel: (01622) 762060 Fax: (01622) 661425

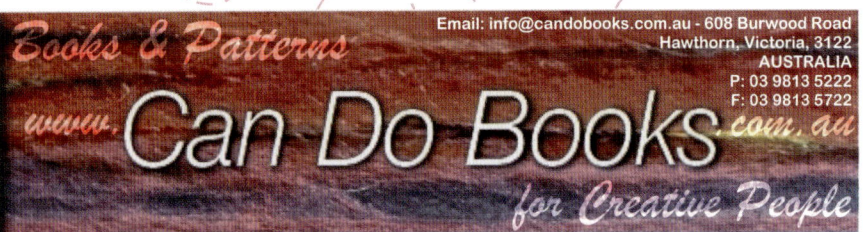

* Needle & Craft
* Woodwork & DIY
* Gardening
* Photography
* Perpetual Patterns

Books & Patterns
www.Can Do Books.com.au
for Creative People

Email: info@candobooks.com.au - 608 Burwood Road
Hawthorn, Victoria, 3122
AUSTRALIA
P: 03 9813 5222
F: 03 9813 5722

The Quilters' Guild

Supporting Quilting and Quilters

Join us - visit www.quiltersguild.org.uk or call 01904 613 242

www.quiltmuseum.org.uk   www.quilltmuseumshop.org.uk

Capricorn are the proud distributors of David & Charles books in Australia

Wholesale enquiries:
E: sales@capricornlink.com.au
T: 00 61 2 4560 1600

More info:
www.capricornlink.com.au

Our quilting titles available for purchase from Highland Quilts www.hqw.com.au

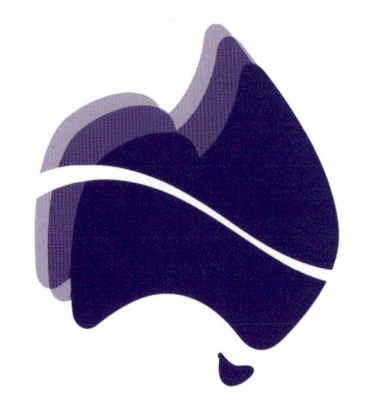

CAPRICORN LINK
AUSTRALIA

www.sewgoodbooks.co.uk

Contact us:
Sewgood Books
Winbow Farm
Washfield
Tiverton
Devon
EX16 9RQ

T: 01398 351160
E: enquiries@sewgoodbooks.co.uk

Sew Good Books

Rhinetex
your specialist in patchwork & quilting

Shop owners can contact us at Rhinetex bv
Geurdeland 7 • 6673 DR Andelst (the Netherlands)
Phone: +31 (0)488 480030 • Fax: +31 (0)488 480422
E-mail: info@rhinetex.com

LECIEN
From our leading supplier Lecien

www.rhinetex.com

The Home Workshop

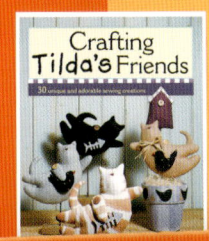

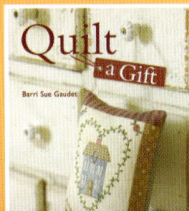

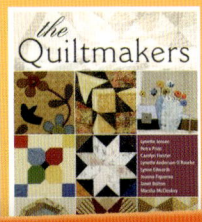

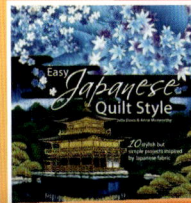

The Home Workshop Books
find us at all the big shows!

post The Home Workshop Ltd
54 Needingworth Road
St Ives
Cambridgeshire
PE27 5JP
UK

phone 01480 465 564

email contactus@thehomeworkshop.co.uk

internet www.thehomeworkshop.co.uk

A DAVID & CHARLES BOOK
Copyright © David & Charles Limited 2010

David & Charles is an F+W Media Inc. company
4700 East Galbraith Road, Cincinnati, OH 45236

First published in the UK in 2010

Text, layout and photography copyright © David & Charles 2010

All rights reserved. No part of this publication may be reproduced, stored in a retrieval system, or transmitted, in any form or by any means, electronic or mechanical, by photocopying, recording or otherwise, without prior permission in writing from the publisher.

A catalogue record for this book is available from the British Library.

ISBN-13: 978-0-7153-3818-6 hardback
ISBN-10: 0-7153-3818-8 hardback

Printed in China by Toppan Leefung Printing Limited
for David & Charles
Brunel House, Newton Abbot, Devon

Photography
The quilts in this diary were beautifully photographed by:
Roger Brown (Ohio Star Sampler); Neil Porter (Up, Out and Into the Light; Purple Prose; Johnson's Floor; Pioneer Patches; Venetian Celebration; Tea Time); David Spaull (Magic Lantern; Flowery Appliqué; Snowball Nine-Patch); Mark Wood (Sampler Quilt; Amish Lilies). All other quilt photographs were taken by Karl Adamson.

Front cover quilt (May Flowers) by Joanne Ridley, photographed by Sian Irvine for *Jelly Roll Inspirations* (Pam & Nicky Lintott, 2009).

Back cover photograph by Sian Irvine for *Two From One Jelly Roll Quilts* (Pam & Nicky Lintott, 2010).

David & Charles publish high quality books on a wide range of subjects. For more great book ideas visit: **www.rucraft.co.uk**